THE

GHOSTLY TALES

OF

DOOR
COUNTY

Published by Arcadia Children's Books
A Division of Arcadia Publishing
Charleston, SC
www.arcadiapublishing.com

Spooky America is a trademark of Arcadia Publishing, Inc.

First published 2021

Manufactured in the United States

ISBN 978-1-4671-9808-0

Library of Congress Control Number: 2021932573

Spooky America

THE GHOSTLY TALES OF DOOR COUNTY

KAREN BUSH GIBSON

Adapted from *Haunted Door County* by Gayle Soucek

arcadia®
CHILDREN'S BOOKS

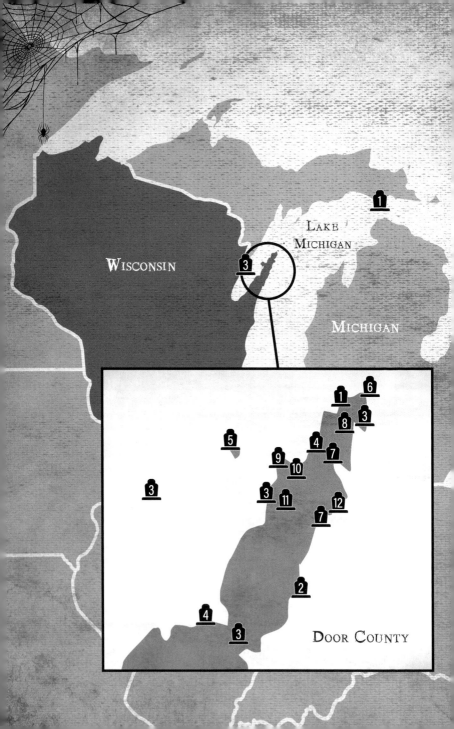

LAKE
MICHIGAN

WISCONSIN

MICHIGAN

DOOR COUNTY

TABLE OF CONTENTS & MAP KEY

Introduction

If you look at a map of Wisconsin, you'll notice a peninsula jutting out from the east side of the state, looking like the gnarled finger of a witch. The peninsula, called the Door Peninsula, is surrounded on three sides by Lake Michigan. Door County gets its name from the peninsula.

The peninsula and county are named after the strait of water at the north end of the peninsula. This watery passageway was once one of the most treacherous stretches of water on the Great Lakes. The French explorers who first saw it and heard of it from the Native people who lived in the area called it *Port des Morts*, or Death's Door. The strait, which links Lake Michigan and Green Bay between the tip of the peninsula and Washington Island, is the site of more freshwater shipwrecks than anywhere else in the world.

Lake Michigan is the second largest of the Great Lakes (after Lake Superior) and the largest lake entirely in the United States. If you think of lakes as pleasant places with calm water for boating and swimming, then Lake Michigan is bound to change your mind.

The weather can change suddenly on the lake. Winds stir up, and waves can reach more than twenty feet high. Strong currents can easily change the course of boats or swimmers. And nowhere has it been more dangerous than in Door County.

Jagged rocks line parts of the coast and the nearby islands. Other rocks hide just below the surface of the water. A fact that many ships discovered too late.

The first known residents were Native Americans, particularly the Potawatomi. Other tribes on the Door Peninsula include the Ho-Chunk (Winnebago), Menominee, and Ojibwe. French explorers arrived in the 1600s, drawn by making their fortunes in the fur trade. But it wasn't until 1844 that white settlers began arriving to stay. Four years later, Wisconsin became a state.

By 1851, there were enough people for most of the peninsula to become an official county— Door County. Although some settlers farmed, the rocky land limited how much they could grow. Many people made a living from lumber or fishing. Others transported the plentiful stone to cities to use for building. And others transported people and cargo from the Door Peninsula to cities such as Milwaukee, Green Bay, or Chicago.

Today, the Door County population is about 30,000, ten times what it was when the county was established. But in the summer, the population swells to around two million. Door County is a popular place to visit. There's plenty to do here—hiking, swimming, and boating. Just keep your eyes open. There are those who refuse to leave. Ever.

Are they Native people caught in canoes when a sudden storm attacked? Maybe nomadic French explorers and trappers who never reached their destinations? Perhaps those who refuse to leave are early settlers who liked Door County so much that they just can't imagine living anywhere else.

The Door County ghosts may reveal themselves as shadows or the bounce of a light. Then there are the unexplained noises that sound like whispers or laughter. You'll feel a sudden chill down your spine. And even though it appears that you're alone, you just can't shake that feeling that someone's watching you.

We look for logical explanations when things like this happen. And perhaps there are answers to why things go bump in the night. But think about this: why have we talked about and studied ghosts for thousands of years?

Many people say they don't believe in ghosts—at least not until they have an encounter with one. Door County is a place where you just might have that encounter. It turns nonbelievers into believers. Maybe it's the rugged coastline with waves crashing into the rocks. Or the isolated back roads away from the crowds. Spooky things happen in Door County, from ghost ships sailing Lake Michigan for eternity to lighthouse keepers who continue their jobs after death. They are joined by early settlers and people who loved the area too much.

In these pages, you'll meet some of Door County's ghosts. But chances are there are many, many more.

The First Ghost
Ship of Door County

Pleasure boats along the coast of Lake Michigan are a common sight. Boaters know to check the weather before going out, but even the most experienced are sometimes caught in an unexpected storm.

This happened to writer Geri Rider in the early 1990s. She and three friends decided to go exploring in a cruiser one day. The waters became noticeable bumpy as they left the safety of the harbor on the west side of the peninsula. Darkening skies followed.

They turned back, struggling to find their way through the rough seas. As they rode the waves up and down, the friends looked for familiar landmarks to tell them where they were. As they topped a wave, Geri spotted a light in front of them. Before her friends could see anything, they had ridden to the bottom of the wave.

As the boat climbed the next wave, all eyes focused ahead of them. And they saw a most unexpected sight. A large wooden ship. And it looked very old. But as quickly as it had appeared, it disappeared into the mist.

The friends eventually made it safely back to their dock. They questioned what they had seen. Had their eyes been playing tricks on them? But Geri and her friends weren't the first to see the ghost ship called *Le Griffon*. It's been making appearances on Lake Michigan for over 340 years.

Le Griffon belonged to France's most famous explorer, Robert LaSalle. He had it built in western New York in 1679 for the purpose of sailing the Great Lakes. In addition to exploring, he wanted to collect furs to pay for more ships, supplies, and crew.

Boats on the Great Lakes were nothing new, but in the 1600s, they were only large lake canoes. *Le Griffon* was unlike anything seen on the Great Lakes before. It was the first full-size sailing ship—forty-five tons!—with multiple sails and seven cannons ready on its deck. It looked like a floating fort.

The masthead on the front of the ship was the mythological beast known as a griffin (also spelled griffon). This animal has the body of a lion and the head of an eagle. Ancient myths say that the griffin is a protector or guardian, especially of treasure or other riches.

Perhaps LaSalle thought it was fitting to have the griffin protect his ship. After all, he did name the ship after this creature. Unfortunately, the griffin wasn't able to protect the ship from Lake Michigan.

On its maiden voyage, *Le Griffon* sailed from Lake Erie. It got the attention of the Iroquois, and a tribal prophet placed a curse on it. As the ship crossed Lake Huron, there were rumors of unhappy crew members. They had worked nonstop through a hard winter to build the ship and ready it for sailing. Some crew members hadn't forgotten the cold and the hunger.

The ship stopped at Mackinac Island, where LaSalle dropped off his lieutenant and about half the crew to prepare for the trip back to New York and a future trip down the Mississippi River.

LaSalle then sailed into Lake Michigan and to Washington Island. (Washington Island is Wisconsin's largest island and is located north of the peninsula.) At this time, the Potawatomi tribe lived in this area. LaSalle greeted Chief Onanguisse. The two leaders had met before and had a good relationship, and LaSalle had come to do business with him. He bought 12,000 pounds of furs from the Potawatomi and paid the tribe with guns, gunpowder, fishhooks, knives, and tools.

LaSalle kept some men with him to explore the Lake Michigan coast and sent *Le Griffon* back to Mackinac Island to pick up the rest of his men and continue on to New York to sell the furs. They would pick him up when they returned.

Le Griffon set sail from Washington Island on September 8, 1679. LaSalle's trusted lieutenant, Henri de Tonti, was at the helm. Father Lewis Hennepin, a French missionary who was traveling on *Le Griffon*, wrote of a "light and favorable wind" as the ship left, firing a cannon in farewell. This was the last time *Le Griffon* was ever seen. It never made it to Mackinac Island.

What happened to *Le Griffon*? No one knows, but there are plenty of guesses, including that curse from the Iroquois prophet. Did another tribe capture the ship and set it on fire? Some Native people whispered that it sailed through a crack in the ice.

In the days of exploration and piracy, some ships had unhappy crew members who weren't treated fairly or wanted a bigger share of treasures. These men would band together and mutiny or take over the ship. For years, there were rumors of a mutiny on *Le Griffon*. Did the crew wreck the ship and steal the furs?

The most popular explanation for the disappearance was that a severe storm sent *Le Griffon* to its icy depths. This is what historians believe today.

Members of the Great Lakes Exploration Group searched for the shipwreck. In 2001, a group of divers saw a bowsprit in the sand. (The bowsprit is the pole that sticks out from the front of the ship.) Years of legal arguments about who owned the remains of *Le Griffon* eventually stopped the search.

The US and French governments and other interested parties finally formed a partnership. The bowsprit was retrieved from the bottom of the lake. It wasn't attached to anything else. We don't even know what century it's from.

We assume *Le Griffon* lies at the bottom of Lake Michigan. Yet with all the technology available, how has the ship avoided discovery for almost 350 years? *Le Griffon* still appears on ghostly voyages, appearing and disappearing in the mist, particularly on stormy nights . . . forever sailing the coast of Door County.

The *Van Valkenburg* Shipwreck

Two hundred years after *Le Griffon* sailed, it was common to see even larger ships making their way along the Great Lakes. One of those ships was the *D.A. Van Valkenburg*, a three-masted ship built in 1866. After many successful journeys, it was overhauled in 1880 so it could have many more.

When the *Van Valkenburg* set out from Chicago in September 1881, no one expected problems. It was just a regular voyage. The ship carried 30,000 bushels of corn and was headed to Buffalo, New York.

The ship left Chicago on a beautiful autumn day. The sun was shining as the *Van Valkenburg* sailed to the center of Lake Michigan. It would keep this course for a while before sailing northeast to Mackinac Island and Lake Huron.

When the *Van Valkenburg* entered Wisconsin waters, things began to change. The sun disappeared behind dark, angry clouds. The gentle breeze they had enjoyed transformed to a gale of unbelievable force. The wind howled and tore into the sails. It tossed the 539-ton ship around like it was a toy.

For two days, the storm continued. Navigating the ship on its original course or even out of the storm was impossible. All the exhausted crew

could do was try to stay afloat and ride out the furious storm.

As night fell on the second day, the ship came to a sudden stop. Over the sounds of pelting rain and howling winds, the crew heard the *Van Valkenburg* groan. Then the ship shuddered.

The storm had tossed the *Van Valkenburg* onto a reef. Through the rain and fog, the crew could make out the dark outline of land nearby.

They had been monitoring the ship's compass and believed they were looking at the Manitou Islands. But they were actually more than fifty miles west from there. The crew was looking at the Door Peninsula on the other side of the lake.

The water between the reef and the land churned dangerously. Waves crashed against the rocks and the ship. Whitecaps glowed in the moonlight. The crew decided to wait until daylight to make their way to land.

Suddenly, the waves began tearing at the ship, ripping it into pieces. As the deck gave way, the crew had no other choice. They had to swim to land. Clinging to pieces of the ship to stay above water, they used every bit of strength to move through the currents. Cries of despair came when they reached land and saw their path blocked by a limestone cliff.

The only way to escape the strong current and punishing waves was to climb this high cliff wall.

The nine crew members tried, over and over again. Exhausted, with waves beating at them, they tried to find handholds and footholds in the cliff. These would either crumble or a particularly strong wave would yank them from the cliff back into the water or tumbling onto rocks below.

Some sailors found twisted cedar trees to hang onto, but the branches were too slippery to hold. The water proved stronger than the crew. One by one, they fell off the cliff, unable to find the strength to continue. With the exception of one.

Thomas Breen was a young crew member. With overpowering determination, he eventually made his way to the top of the wall. He collapsed, but not for long. Somehow, he found the strength to get to his feet and look for help.

Bloody and battered, Thomas limped a couple of miles to the nearest town, Jacksonport. By morning, the townspeople rushed to help the remaining survivors, but there were none.

Four bodies were found on shore. The other four were never seen again. The shore was littered with pieces of the ship and thousands of bushels of corn.

Today, if you visit the site, you may still see the wooden decking from the ship just a short distance from shore. As darkness arrives, people often see and hear even more: dark shapes struggling in the water and tortured voices crying out for help. Nonbelievers say it's the seagulls or the wind. Others insist it's the suffering seamen crying out to be saved.

Not long ago, a young couple was driving south from Jacksonport to Sturgeon Bay one evening. The road had lots of curves and was lined with thick stands of trees, which formed a canopy over the road.

As their car drove around one of these curves, their headlights caught the sight of a man struggling to walk along the side of the road. They pulled up next to the man, noticing his clothing ripped to shreds. He was also dripping wet, even though it wasn't raining.

The woman lowered her car window to ask if he needed them to call for help. When he turned toward them, they gasped at his bruised and bloody face. Sad eyes looked at them for a few seconds before he vanished.

The couple sped away. After they calmed down, they questioned what they had seen. The clothing looked old and out of place. And had they really been able to see moonlight *through* this man? Had he really vanished into thin air? They didn't want to believe it. Worried that the man might have been a victim of a horrible accident, they turned around. They drove all the way to Jacksonport, looking for a man who might need help. They never found him.

So, if you're driving one evening from Jacksonport to Sturgeon Bay, maybe you'll see Thomas Breen, still trying to find help for his *Van Valkenburg* crewmates.

Egg Harbor Express

In May 1986, a funeral for two people was held in Sturgeon Bay, the county seat of Door County. The bodies were carried in handmade oak coffins in a horse-drawn hearse that dated from 1898. While handmade coffins and horse-drawn hearses aren't common, they aren't what is most unusual about this story. There were no names for those being buried. While also unusual, that's not what makes this story so special—and spooky.

What is most unusual about this funeral was that the deceased had died almost eighty-three years earlier. They were two of eleven people who died in the 1903 shipwreck of the *Erie L. Hackley*. The passenger steamer was on its way to Egg Harbor when it perished on the west side of the Door Peninsula.

The *Hackley* was a small steamer boat that had been transporting passengers and mail around Lake Michigan for over twenty years. You see, it was easier and faster to travel Door County by boat in those early days. Remember, this was very rocky land. When you traveled by horse-drawn cart or coach, the bumps and bouncing were almost unbearable.

Captain Joseph Vorous of Fish Creek had suggested starting a passenger service in the Green Bay area of Lake Michigan. He and three other men opened the Fish Creek Transportation

Company in the spring of 1903. They purchased the *Hackley* and began hauling passengers on a daily thirty-five-mile route that crossed the bay.

With Vorous as the *Hackley* captain and another partner, Orin Rowin, serving as engineer, the seventy-nine-foot wooden steamer left Sturgeon Bay each day, crossing the lake to Menominee in Michigan. Then it traveled back to Egg Harbor before turning north to stop at Fish Creek and then Washington Island.

People got used to seeing the small steamer moving back and forth on its daily runs and nicknamed it the "Egg Harbor Express." By that summer, many of the western Door County residents had enjoyed trips on the Egg Harbor Express.

Yet when September came, the *Hackley* spent more time at the dock than the open water. First, it had a damaged propeller shaft. Two weeks after that, there was trouble with the boiler. Like the propeller, the boiler supplied power to move the boat through the water. After the propeller and boiler were repaired, a few days of dangerous winds kept the *Hackley* from going out.

On Saturday, October 3, it appeared that the *Hackley* would finally be able to make its regular journey. In addition to its passengers, it had quite a bit of cargo because it had been off the water for so long.

On the journey to Menominee, the water grew rougher as southwest winds blew. Passengers and cargo were dropped off at Menominee, while more boarded for the trip to Egg Harbor and then Fish Creek. When they set sail from Menominee at 5:45 p.m., there were nineteen crew and passengers on board.

There were supposed to be twenty, but Edgar Thorp, one of the co-owners, decided at the last minute to stay in Menominee instead. He was very uneasy about making the trip across the lake. The weather forecast predicted a cold front and possible strong winds from the northwest. But

Captain Vorous believed they could make the trip across the lake before bad weather hit.

As the Egg Harbor Express made its way back across the lake, Captain Vorous and the crew watched the sky to the north. They were totally unprepared when a monstrous gale hit them from behind. The already rough waters became worse, battering the small boat and causing it to lean dangerously in the water.

Vorous aimed the boat for Green Island, midway between Menominee and Egg Harbor. As the passengers rushed to the life preservers, a monstrous wave hit the *Hackley*, ripping the pilot house from the steamer. Thousands of gallons of water filled the hull, dragging the boat down to the bottom of the bay. It all happened in less than two minutes.

While some drowned immediately, others found something to hold onto. Passengers and crew spent the night being tossed about in the icy water. By morning, only eight people were still alive.

When the Egg Harbor Express hadn't arrived by morning, search parties went out looking for her. Another steamer, the *Sheboygan*, knew nothing about the *Hackley*. It had waited out the storm at Washington Island and was now behind schedule. A passenger called to Captain Asa Johnson about seeing something in the water.

Captain Johnson reached for his binoculars to take a closer look. To his surprise, he saw people hanging onto debris. He swung the *Sheboygan* around and rescued four passengers and four crewmen.

Efforts at retrieving the boat or the remains of the passengers and crew were unsuccessful until June 1980—seventy-seven years after the *Hackley* sank. Modern equipment allowed searchers to find the *Hackley* two miles north of Green Island. All they could retrieve were the two skeletons, identities unknown, that received the special burial six years later.

Captain Vorous and deckhand Freeman Thorp are among those with tombstones at the Pioneer Cemetery in Fish Creek, but their graves are believed to be empty. However, people report that that the two men wander between the shoreline and the cemetery on stormy nights, particularly in the autumn. Are they looking for the *Hackley*? Searching for survivors?

Other people report hearing screams from the open water. Are these shrieks from ghosts of the Egg Harbor Express? Still hoping to be saved from a watery grave?

Experienced sailors reportedly avoid sailing on the north side of Green Island. They don't explain why, but for some reason, they prefer not to take the route of the doomed Egg Harbor Express . . .

Lighthouse on Sturgeon Bay

Sherwood Point
Minnie

For all the shipwrecks that have happened near the Door Peninsula, many more have been avoided because of lighthouses. Lighthouses guide ships through dangerous areas. Perhaps it's not surprising then that Door County's lighthouses have their share of ghosts, too.

By the 1800s, there was a lot of ship traffic on Lake Michigan. Corn, wheat, and other goods were transported from Chicago to Green Bay. Stone and timber for building were transported from Green Bay to Chicago. The most difficult part of the trip was passing through the dangerous Death's Door or traveling farther north to avoid it.

Midway down the Door Peninsula, a shallow marsh known as Sturgeon Bay reaches across almost the entire peninsula, except for about a mile of sand. Native people once used this to get from one side of Lake Michigan to the other. They sailed as far as they could and then carried their canoes the remainder of the way.

In the 1870s, Joseph Harris Sr., publisher of the *Sturgeon Bay* newspaper, had the idea of making a shipping channel through Sturgeon Bay. Not only would the channel help ships avoid Death's Door, it would also take 200 miles off the journey.

In 1878, the channel was complete enough for small ships to pass through. And more than four hundred did just that in the first year. By late September, the Sherwood Point Lighthouse had been built on the limestone cliffs of the western shore to help ships find their way into the bay. Unlike other Door County lighthouses, which were built with cream-colored bricks, this one was built with red bricks, and its thirty-five-foot tower was fitted with a Fresnel lens that could cast a light up to fourteen miles away.

The first lighthouse keeper was Henry Stanley. He and his wife, Katherine, were experienced lighthouse keepers. But the Sherwood Point Lighthouse was a challenge. Unlike other local lighthouses that displayed just a fixed white beacon, the Sherwood Point beacon was designed to also flash a red light every minute. This mechanism worked like a clock, but the clock kept breaking down. The clock repairman was a frequent visitor at the lighthouse.

During the second year at Sherwood Point, Katherine's niece joined them. Twenty-one-year-old Minnie Hesh was from Brooklyn, New York, and had recently lost her parents. She was a big help to her aunt and uncle. Not only was she a cheerful presence, but she also helped take care of the lighthouse.

Minnie wrote in the logbook and helped keep the clockwork and beacon working. After several years, she met and married William Cochems, who ran the town's hardware store. Although Minnie moved in with her new husband, she still helped her aunt and uncle when she could.

By 1894, a fog bell had been added to Henry Stanley's duties. It had to be wound by hand every four hours. Henry was now seventy years old, and Katherine's health was poor, so they were having trouble keeping up with all the work.

Henry received permission to hire an official assistant. He hired Minnie's husband. William had no lighthouse experience, but we suspect Minnie and Henry taught him everything he needed to know. When Henry died a year later, William took over as keeper. Katherine was named assistant keeper. As a widow, she needed the income. Eventually Katherine moved to town, and Minnie was named the official assistant lighthouse keeper, a position she held for the rest of her life.

Minnie continued to work hard at Sherwood Point. In addition to lighthouse duties, she kept a clean house and planted a garden. Sherwood Point

was always ready for friends and visitors. And there were many. Minnie would bring out her fine china to serve tea and something to eat. It was a happy place.

On an August morning in 1928, Minnie rose from bed and collapsed. She died of a sudden heart attack. William was heartbroken. You can still see the memorial he built for her in her garden.

In 1939, the lighthouse was turned over to the US Coast Guard. This branch of the US military is charged with keeping our coastlines and waterways safe. Yet the Coast Guard officers assigned to Sherwood Point soon learned that they had company. *Ghostly* company. They could dismiss what sounded like footsteps on the stairs or a sudden cold breeze indoors as tricks of the wind. But what about the laughter? Or when it sounded like a tea party was happening? And no breeze through an open window can make a bed.

The Sherwood Point light was automated in 1983, so keepers are no longer needed there. The

Coast Guard still maintains the property, and it has been turned into a vacation spot for Coast Guard members and their families.

Everyone knows about Minnie. She's mentioned often in the Sherwood Point guest logs. The Coast Guard once invited eight paranormal investigators to the lighthouse to see what they could find. Although each of the eight heard a woman laughing and talking, they were unable to record the sound. And the video equipment they brought malfunctioned at critical times.

On another occasion, a Coast Guardsman and his wife came to visit. After dinner, they headed out to see the sights of the Door County coast. When they returned later that night, they were too tired to clean up the kitchen and decided to wait until morning. They went to bed.

The couple woke suddenly to sounds of footsteps, laughter, and the rattling of dishes in the kitchen. They were frozen with fear. Finally, the husband called out.

"Minnie. If you're going to make so much noise with the dishes, you could at least wash them!"

The noises stopped, and the couple fell asleep. When they woke the next morning, they decided

they had imagined the noises from the night before. That is, until they went to the kitchen. The dishes from last night's dinner were washed and put away. The kitchen was spotless. All except for a single teacup and saucer sitting on the edge of the table.

Minnie still enjoys receiving guests, even though she's been dead for almost 100 years. She takes care of the lighthouse and all who enter.

CHAPTER
5

Chambers Island Lighthouse

As lighthouses along the Door County coast became automated, many fell into ruin with no one to look after them. This seemed to be the fate of the Chambers Island Lighthouse in 1976, when the Coast Guard transferred ownership of the more-than-one-hundred-year-old lighthouse to Gibraltar Township.

The township turned the lighthouse grounds into a forty-acre park. The lighthouse is open for tours when the caretakers are in residence during the summer months.

The first caretakers, Joel and Mary Blahnik, had a lot of work to do when they were first hired. Joel, a former Coast Guard captain, had lived in Door County his entire life. Restoring the Chambers Island Lighthouse to its former glory sounded like a challenge he could handle. He just never expected the "help" he would receive.

During the first year at the island, the Blahniks were busy clearing debris from the lighthouse. On that first day, Joel had help from his nine-year-old son. They were exhausted by the time they crawled into their sleeping bags in a first-floor bedroom. Sleep came quickly.

Joel woke suddenly to the definite sound of heavy footsteps on the cast-iron lighthouse stairs. Glancing next to him, he saw his son sleeping deeply. The footsteps continued. Joel realized they were coming down the hallway toward the bedroom. He held his breath until the footsteps were past the bedroom. The footsteps continued through the living room on their way to the kitchen. Joel heard the kitchen door opening and closing.

The caretaker leaped up, ready to confront the intruder. He went out the kitchen door that led to an old strawberry garden. Joel found no one. In fact, it was eerily quiet.

As the season at the lighthouse continued with no more incidents, Joel thought perhaps he had imagined the sounds from that first night. Sure, occasionally, he felt like he wasn't alone, but that was probably just the sounds of an old house.

The next spring, Joel again arrived at the Chambers Island Lighthouse to prepare it for opening. The first night, he was bedded down in a first-floor bedroom when he again heard heavy footsteps coming down the stairs, walking past his room, through the kitchen, and out the back door.

This time, Joel sprang up quickly in order to catch this night visitor. But when he arrived at the old strawberry garden area, it was again empty. Suddenly, Joel realized that the intruder was no intruder at all. It was just Lewis Williams, handing off the care of his beloved Chambers Island Lighthouse to Joel.

Lewis Williams was the first and longest-serving keeper at Chambers Island Lighthouse. Before this, he owned and ran a sawmill. But Lewis had two things in his favor: he loved Chambers Island, where he had lived for twenty years, and it was his land on which the lighthouse was built.

Chambers Island is the largest of a cluster of islands in Green Bay. In the mid-1800s, it was populated by fishermen and lumbermen. In the winter months, when the bay froze over, people took horse-drawn sleigh rides to the mainland for supplies. In the early spring and late fall, people stayed off the lake to avoid the dangerous sheets and chunks of ice floating in the bay.

With more shipping on Green Bay and Lake Michigan, locals decided a lighthouse was needed on the west side of the island to help ships along the channel between Chambers Island and the Upper Michigan shore. The other channel between the island and Door County—Strawberry Channel— was only seven miles wide and rocky. Bigger ships avoided it.

Lewis sold forty acres of a small peninsula jutting from the northwest side of the island for $250. It was the perfect place for a lighthouse. And it's suspected that part of the deal was that Lewis would be the keeper.

In 1868, construction began on the cream-colored Milwaukee brick lighthouse. The first two levels of the sixty-eight-foot tower were square. The top two levels were in the shape of an octagon.

The beacon first shone its light over the water in October of that year. Lewis moved in with his wife and eleven children. He learned what he needed to know and took excellent care of the lighthouse for twenty-one years.

Lewis was known as an excellent host. He had planted a strawberry patch outside his kitchen door. Strawberries were a particular treat when Chambers Island was cut off from the mainland. And his wife made strawberry pies and preserves that were the talk of the island.

Seven keepers followed Lewis after he retired in 1889, but none remained as long as he did. Eventually the lighthouse was automated in 1955. Six years later, a ninety-seven-foot metal tower, with a solar-powered light, was built closer to the water.

Fast forward to the 1970s. After a couple of years of the Blahniks being in charge of the lighthouse, Lewis became more helpful. Or perhaps playful. One day, Joel was working on a window. He set his screwdriver on the windowsill. When he reached for it again, it was gone. Joel looked around on the ground, certain that it had rolled off, but couldn't find it. Later, the screwdriver was found under a pillow in one of the bedrooms.

Other tools went missing only to later turn up in the oddest places. There were also a few instances of beds being shaken in the middle of the night. Joel and his wife never felt threatened. Lewis was just having a good time.

This continued, and several years later, a group of nuns came to tour the lighthouse one day. Joel mentioned his ghostly visitor to the nuns. At the top of the lighthouse tower, one of the nuns began praying for Lewis's soul to be released from this earth.

Since that time, there have been no sounds of Lewis's footsteps moving through the lighthouse. No tools go missing. No shaking beds. But occasionally, you find yourself looking around for someone who isn't there. And is that the smell of strawberries in the air? Lewis was such a dedicated lighthouse keeper that we doubt he's gone for good. Perhaps he's just taking a break and causing mischief somewhere else. But he'll be back. The question is when. What do you think?

Lake Michigan, Door County

Rock Island Shadows

Rock Island is a small island a mile northeast of Washington Island. It is the northernmost point of Door County. Today, it is Rock Island State Park, with no cars allowed. Visitors are welcome between Memorial Day and early October and can take a ferry there from Washington Island. No one lives permanently at Rock Island—at least no one *living*.

People report strange things on Rock Island: shadows moving through the woods; the feeling that someone—or some*thing*—is moving by your side, but when you turn, no one is there; whispers, chanting. Others report the sounds of children laughing and playing but seeing no one there.

In the mid-1600s, the only residents of the island were members of the Potawatomi (sometimes spelled Pottawatomie) tribe. Other tribes and early European settlers left them alone in this isolated place, since the canoe ride between Rock Island and Washington Island was dangerous due to turbulent water. But by the early 1800s, the Potawatomi began seeing more and more Europeans sail by their island. Some stopped and stayed. One of the first European settlements in Door County was a fishing village on the east side of Rock Island.

Around 1832, businessmen began pushing for a lighthouse to be built to help guide ships through the Rock Island Passage north of the island. Work began in 1836. The lighthouse was operational the next year. The Pottawatomie Lighthouse, sitting on top of a 147-foot bluff at the northwest tip of the island, was the first lighthouse on Lake Michigan and in the state of Wisconsin.

David Corbin, born in Vermont, was hired as the first keeper. As a young man, he fought in the War of 1812. He came to Rock Island with his dog and a horse named Jock. The isolation of this station was difficult for this shy man. It didn't help that the lighthouse was poorly built. Plaster fell from the walls and ceiling. The mortar that held the bricks and stone together cracked, allowing water and icy winds to make their way indoors. It made Pottawatomie Lighthouse a gloomy place to live.

David had few visitors. Occasionally, he saw fishermen or one of the families who lived on the other side of the island. But he was lonely. The lighthouse inspector who visited David in 1845 was concerned. He gave David twenty days off to "go out and find a wife."

Unfortunately, David was unsuccessful in finding a wife to share his life at the lighthouse. Yet by

1850, a woman and her three children had moved in, and a laborer reportedly lived here as well.

David didn't have long to enjoy his company. Years of dampness and some particularly hard winters caused his health to decline. He died in December 1852 at the age of fifty-seven.

You'll find David's grave in a small cemetery south of the lighthouse. He had served as Pottawatomie Lighthouse keeper for fifteen years. Four other keepers worked here but none for as long. Perhaps they were overwhelmed by the gloom and fled.

Finally, in 1858, the Lighthouse Board built a new and improved lighthouse. About a dozen more  lighthouse keepers passed through until the light was automated in 1946. It is now the Pottawatomie Lighthouse Museum.

Volunteers stay here during the season from Memorial Day to early October. They give tours of the lighthouse. If you ask, maybe they'll tell you about the frequent ghostly footsteps or the doors opening and closing. It appears that David is pleased with the renovations and the company. You might even see a shadowy figure in the lantern room. It's just David Corbin, still taking care of his lighthouse.

Spooky Wheels Go Round and Round

You've heard about the ghostly ships of Door County. Would it surprise you to know that not all of the spooky sounds and sights belong to ships or even to once-living human beings? Sometimes, things like bicycles and cars from long ago make ghostly appearances. At least in Door County, they do.

Door County has many scenic roads, but one of the most talked about is Ridges Road in Baileys

Harbor, a pretty harbor on the east side of the peninsula. This stretch of road runs along the Lake Michigan shoreline on the north side of the bay.

The forest of cedar, pine, maple, and other trees is so thick that it blocks views of the lake. Instead, a green canopy stretches over the road during the spring and summer. The canopy turns gold and orange in the autumn, and fallen leaves blanket the road.

If you traveled along the road at night, maybe you heard something odd. It started with strangely familiar soft squeaks and rattles. As the sounds came closer, they got louder. They were the sounds of a bicycle that desperately needed to be oiled.

You turned around toward the sound, ready to greet the rider. All you saw was a very old bicycle moving down the road. If you saw the rider of the bicycle, it was an older man with a bushy mustache wearing some type of uniform. He rides past you and into the mist just ahead.

This ghostly rider was the last commander of the Baileys Harbor Life-Saving Station. He lived in a nearby cabin. And if you stop to have a look at the cabin in the daytime, you'll see that same bicycle leaning against the gray, weathered outer walls of the cabin.

The US government started lifesaving stations in 1848 to aid ships in distress. These stations started along the East Coast and then spread to the Great Lakes. Wisconsin had twelve, with four of them in Door County.

In forty years, the Baileys Harbor Station responded to 465 calls for help, saving many lives. Lifesaving stations eventually evolved into the

US Coast Guard. During World War II, the men from the Baileys Harbor Station were assigned to search and rescue operations in the North Atlantic Ocean.

After the war, the Baileys Harbor Station returned to helping boats and ships in need on Lake Michigan. And it was during this time that the station commander rode his bicycle on Ridges Road.

Eventually, Coast Guard boats and equipment improved so much that the stations were no longer needed. The Baileys Harbor Station closed, and the land was sold. Most of the buildings were torn down, except for the little cabin once occupied by the commander. Townhomes, cabins, and a marina were built, and the commander's cabin was used as a storage shed by a land developer. And for a long time, an old bicycle rested up against the cabin and people spotted the ghost of the station commander riding his bicycle on Ridges Road.

When the developer heard about the ghostly bicycle, he had the bicycle cleaned up and painted white. Then he placed the bicycle back against the station commander's old cabin. Since then, there have been no more sightings of a ghostly bicycle on Ridges Road. Is the ghost rider angry about the changes to his bicycle? Perhaps. Or maybe he's taking care of other station duties. But some night when the moon is just right, he'll take his bicycle out again for a spin on Ridges Road.

As familiar as the sounds of a squeaky bicycle are, so are the sounds of a car engine—particularly an old car. The engine chugs as it works to power the vehicle. There's usually some bouncing and squeaks too.

People traveling on the Washington Island Ferry or in a pleasure boat have heard these sounds on the lake. The sounds are most often heard during the winter when the water is calmer. And if you listen very carefully, you might hear the sounds of crunching ice or teenage boys whooping and hollering.

Washington Island is the only island in Door County where people live year-round. The infamous Death's Door stretches between the island and the mainland. When cold north winds from Canada blow in, the deep blue water turns to ice.

For the past seventy years or so, icebreaker boats have cleared the ice, allowing people to get to the mainland. In the early years of settlement, people rode horse-drawn sleighs and sleds across the frozen bay. Then snowmobiles and cars drove along rough ice roads.

Even frozen, Death's Door was considered a dangerous route because of the current and rocks. Many people took a longer but safer route west of the island.

In 1935, Washington Island's boys' basketball team was having a great season. They were invited to play in a tournament in Ellison Bay on the mainland. A caravan of cars with players and fans took the long route across the frozen lake. They were led by the basketball coach, Ralph Wade, driving a two-door Ford Model A sedan.

The boys won the tournament and spent the night on the mainland. The next morning, the group was to gather and head back home to Washington Island. However, several people didn't show up.

Coach Wade owned a tavern on Washington Island. He was in a hurry to get back and open it for his regular customers, as he knew they'd want to hear how the team had done. At 11:30 a.m., he decided to go ahead and leave with five of his star basketball players.

When the rest of the group got back to Washington Island, they learned that the tavern hadn't been opened. And no one had seen the coach or boys. Search parties formed and carefully made their way across the ice. They discovered a large, jagged hole near Plum Island along Death's Door. Rather than taking the safer route, Coach Wade had taken the dangerous shortcut across the lake. Even frozen, Death's Door wasn't safe.

The Coast Guard arrived with icebreaking equipment and began dragging the lake. After a few days, they made a grim discovery. They located the Ford Model A. Squeezed in the back seat were the bodies of three of the boys. The Coast Guard

continued looking. They eventually found the bodies of the other two boys and Coach Wade.

Instead of celebrating a tournament championship, Washington Island held funerals and grieved the loss of Coach Wade and five boys.

Even eighty-five years later, this tragic loss hasn't been forgotten. How can it be, when people continue to hear an old engine chugging away on a journey across Death's Door? If you listen carefully, you'll also hear the sounds of laughter. It sounds just like a car full of teenagers celebrating.

The Milkmaid
and the Barman

Ghosts tend to hang around specific places. Interestingly enough, it's rarely cemeteries. Instead, ghosts are often found in places where the person once lived or spent a lot of time. Washington Island's ghosts are no exception.

Washington Island isn't only Door County's largest island, it also has the largest settlement of Icelanders outside of Iceland. And many Scandinavian immigrants moved to the island because it reminded them of the homes they had left behind. Since there were so many Scandinavian immigrants, there are bound to be Scandinavian ghosts.

One of these is a tall, young blonde woman who walks along Range Line Road. In the early 20th century, this was an area of dairy farms. This spirit is dressed like an old-fashioned milkmaid, and she carries a milk pail in each hand. She is often described as having no legs, or her legs are hidden behind a thick mist. Soon after this ghostly milkmaid is seen, she disappears in the trees.

People refer to her as Gretchen, although no one is certain of her name or who she was. Because little is known about her, there are different tales about her life. One story says that she was an immigrant brought to work on a farm in the early 1900s and was a hardworking, valued employee. Another version claims she was mistreated and was trying to run away.

THE MILKMAID AND THE BARMAN

Her lack of legs is explained as the result of an accident. It is believed that Gretchen, carrying pails full of milk, walked into the road without looking. She was struck down by either a horse-drawn carriage or perhaps an automobile. She lost her legs in the accident, and a few days later, she lost her life.

Even though we don't know who Gretchen is, hopefully someday she will find eternal peace. Until then, she is determined to carry the milk to its destination.

We do know a little more about another Scandinavian ghost, Tom Nelson. Born in Denmark, he immigrated to Washington Island in the 1890s. Around the turn of the century, he built a saloon at Detroit Harbor in the southwest part of the island. It was named Nelsen's Hall. (For some reason, Tom's last name and the name of the

69

saloon are spelled differently.) Tom was a friendly man. He was often heard to say, "You're only a stranger here but once."

In 1920, the 18th Amendment was passed, outlawing the sale of alcohol. The law, known as Prohibition, was in place for thirteen years. Most saloons were forced to close, but not Nelsen's Hall.

Federal revenue agents eventually raided Nelsen's Hall. Tom was ready for them. He explained that he operated a pharmacy and showed his pharmacist license. It was legitimate. The only alcohol he sold was something known as Angostura bitters. Bitters are added to cocktails to give them flavor.

Tom claimed that the alcohol he served was medicine. And in fact, a doctor first invented it as medicine. Tom brought the town doctor over,

 who explained to the agents that bitters were known to relieve stomach problems. Apparently, a lot of people on Washington Island, including Tom,

had stomach problems. There was little the agents could do.

Tom lived to the age of eighty-nine. When he died, he passed the saloon on to family members, who ran it until 1973. Since then, it's passed through many hands. It's been a dance hall, an ice cream parlor, and a movie theater.

The present owners purchased it in 1999 and returned it to its roots—a saloon and restaurant. And apparently Tom is still hanging around. Unexplained temperature drops and things being moved are common occurrences. The sound of footsteps and doors slamming are often heard. Sometimes there are voices too. One of the co-owners once heard a man ask for a glass of water at the bar. When she turned around with the water, no one was there.

Seems like Tom loved his saloon and serving the folks of Detroit Harbor so much that he can't bring himself to leave. He still wants everyone to feel welcome.

CHAPTER 9

Alexander Noble House

Anyone who has ever watched a scary movie or celebrated Halloween knows about haunted houses. And yes, Door County has those too. One of the best known is the Alexander Noble House in the town of Fish Creek. Operated by the Gibraltar Historical Association, it's open to the public.

Alexander Noble was a successful Scottish immigrant. He first lived on Chambers Island, where he started a lumber mill. But he didn't like the isolation of the island, so he moved his wife and three children across the water to Fish Creek in 1862.

Fish Creek was a town that was quickly growing. This was largely due to Asa Thorp. Asa built a sturdy dock, inviting passing ships to stop. He sold barrels to merchants, fishermen, and lumbermen. Some of them decided to stay in Fish Creek.

When Noble decided to move to Fish Creek, it already had three general stores, churches, a school, and a library. He staked a claim on 300 acres east of town. Noble grew crops like peas and corn. He also had some livestock. He became the town blacksmith as well. He shoed horses, made tools, and fixed things.

Sadly, Alexander's wife, Emily, died in 1873. Later that year, the Noble's log farmhouse burned down. Although no one was hurt, he lost mementos of his first marriage. Alexander eventually remarried, and he and his new wife, Maria, had four children.

The entire family moved to town, where Alexander bought a lot from Asa Thorp in the center of town. Instead of the usual log cabins people lived in, Alexander built a Greek Revival–style home. It was the grandest house in Fish Creek. Its large covered porch and beautiful gardens encouraged people to stop by and visit.

Alexander became interested in local politics and served in a few positions before being named postmaster. The post office was actually located in the front parlor of his grand house.

Alexander Noble died in 1903; Maria lived until 1932. Their granddaughter, Dr. Gertrude Howe, inherited the home. She served as a family doctor and saw patients at the house. After her death in 1995, the Gibraltar Historical Association acquired the property.

The Alexander Noble House was a treasure trove for the historical association. Apparently, the Noble family didn't throw things away. There were old blacksmith tools, papers, and medical equipment, including the skeleton Gertrude used to study anatomy. The association displayed these things when it opened the house as a museum. What the association didn't plan on was the help it would receive in greeting visitors.

Stand outside the home for a few minutes. Pay particular attention to the upstairs windows facing Main Street. If you see someone looking out the window, don't assume it's another visitor. Take a closer look. If you see a distinguished gentleman in old-fashioned clothes or a woman dressed in white lace, then you are probably seeing Alexander or Maria Noble. They enjoy watching the activity on Main Street.

Strange noises and voices are often heard in the house. Footsteps are common. Occasionally, lights flicker and picture frames fall from the wall. But what is most startling is when you look in one of the original downstairs mirrors. Don't be surprised if you see a woman in Victorian dress pass by behind you or a man looking into the mirror next to you.

Look for mist in the backyard. If you see some, watch it for a while. Many people have reported seeing a woman dressed in white and carrying a baby in the mist. People report that great sadness comes with this vision. She is Alexander's first wife, Emily. Apparently, even though her home burned down, she moved with the family into their new house in town. Emily's three children claimed that their mother used to call to them from the backyard garden when they were young. Her ghost often approaches the back door with her arms out as if handing off a bundle to someone before she disappears.

Every few years, the association holds a Victorian-age funeral for Alexander. As was the custom, mirrors and windows are covered. Clocks are stopped. A casket sits in the front parlor as a horse-drawn hearse waits outside.

Photos taken during the event often show many orbs of light dancing around the casket. Once, a nearby chair appeared to burst into flames. Yet a second look showed the chair unharmed.

Emily, Alexander, and Maria Noble are buried in a family plot in a nearby cemetery. However, it appears they would rather remain in the house, welcoming their visitors.

Eagle Bluff Lighthouse

Haunted Huey

We've met Asa Thorp. Now it's time to meet one of his relatives. Asa's great-nephew, Huey Melvin, was born in Fish Creek. The town and the shore up to the Eagle Bluff Lighthouse was six-year-old Huey's playground. He knew everyone, and everyone knew him.

The friendly blond boy greeted passengers from the steamer arriving for a summer visit. Huey probably told the summer visitors that he would be starting school in the fall. Huey was looking forward to seeing where the big kids spent their days.

But in late July, Huey got sick. It started with muscle aches. And then a fever. He became weaker and weaker. Huey had tetanus, a bacterial infection that usually starts from a puncture wound made by something like a rusty nail.

Today, we all get vaccinated for tetanus. But in 1904, that wasn't possible. Huey died, and the community was heartbroken. They buried him in Pioneer Cemetery, where other family members were buried. It's not far from Huey's beloved lighthouse.

Pioneer Cemetery is now hidden in the forests of Peninsula State Park, just north of Fish Creek. If you can find the cemetery, you can find Huey's grave. The headstone is topped with a lamb.

Many families still visit Door County in the summer. One family in particular used to camp at Peninsula State Park every summer. They discovered Pioneer Cemetery and Huey's grave. It became a family tradition to greet Huey after they arrived at the park.

The family visited one summer after there had been heavy rains. With the ground too muddy for camping, they checked into a cabin at the Thorp House Inn instead. What they didn't know was that Huey had lived and died nearby.

One night, the parents were awakened by a soft knock on their bedroom door. Thinking it was one of their children, the father called out, but was answered only by a sudden icy chill. The parents then watched as a mist formed at the foot of their bed. The mist transformed into a small blond boy, dressed in an old-fashioned white sleep shirt.

The boy moved to the door. He turned back to the couple and waved his hand as if to say, "Come with me." Then he disappeared. The couple tried to convince themselves that it was some sort of strange dream. But the second night, it happened again.

The next morning, their young daughter mentioned she had seen Huey the previous night. Her parents questioned her. The daughter said she had fun talking and playing with him in her room.

Suddenly it made sense! The parents realized that the boy they had seen was the same one whose grave they usually visited. But this year, because of the rain, they hadn't. Huey had come to see them. They immediately went to the cemetery and paid their respects. They saw no more of Huey on that visit.

But Huey has been seen by many other people, including a Peninsula State Park ranger. The ranger was on patrol one evening when he saw a small boy on the side of the road. He looked around but didn't see anyone with him. Why would a young boy be on his own in the woods? Perhaps his family was camping nearby.

The park ranger pulled up alongside Huey and lowered his window. He asked him if his parents were around. Huey took off through the woods. The park ranger called out to him, but he kept running toward the lighthouse. The park ranger knew the bluff wasn't safe for a young boy at night.

He drove to the lighthouse, looking for the boy. As he pulled up to the lighthouse, the boy burst through the woods, heading toward the lighthouse. The park ranger called out. This time, Huey stopped and turned toward the ranger.

Before the ranger could question the boy, he noticed the old-fashioned clothes the boy wore: short woolen pants and a white ruffled shirt. Even stranger, the park ranger could see the lighthouse brick *through* the boy. Huey then turned and disappeared into the brick.

Huey is often seen playing near the cemetery or the lighthouse. In fact, Huey has become somewhat of an unofficial ambassador, welcoming people to Fish Creek and Peninsula State Park. And he's developed quite a following. People often leave things at his grave—small toys, shiny coins, and other gifts. Perfect gifts for a boy who likes to have fun and who will forever be six years old.

CHAPTER 11

Eerie Egg Harbor

Egg Harbor lies south of Fish Creek. One of Egg Harbor's oldest buildings is now home to a restaurant called Shipwrecked, and it's also home to quite a few ghosts.

If you spot a rude logger, then you're probably looking at a resident of the Kewaunee Boarding House. That was what the building originally was when it was constructed in the 1800s. Lumbermen and sailors rented rooms here.

You might see a woman in Victorian dress near the front door. The building was the Harbor Inn when she first began waiting for a stagecoach over a hundred years ago.

Once, a visitor to Egg Harbor was outside Shipwrecked when he noticed a boy on the roof. Frightened that the boy might fall, the police were called, yet no boy was ever found. That's because the boy, Jason, had died decades ago.

Jason is believed to be the son of the infamous Al Capone, also known as "Scarface Al." Capone was a larger-than-life gangster who worked out of Chicago. But even gangsters like to get away, and one of Capone's favorite spots was in the building where Shipwrecked is today. Back then, in the 1920s, it was called Murphy's. Capone enjoyed the peaceful, scenic location. An added bonus was that Murphy's provided a built-in escape route.

The basement stairs led to underground tunnels, part of the Horseshoe Bay Natural Cavern, the

EERIE EGG HARBOR

second largest cave in Wisconsin. If Capone needed to make a getaway, the tunnels could carry him to the beach, where he had a speed boat waiting.

Jason knew his father was a gangster, and he didn't like the way his father treated his mother. Jason hoped that if he gathered enough incriminating evidence against his dad and turned it over to authorities, perhaps Capone would go to jail. And his mom would not have to put up with him anymore. But Capone found out about Jason's plans—and Jason was found dead shortly thereafter.

Another frequent ghostly visitor is Verna Moore, the wife of Murphy Moore, the former owner of Murphy's. Verna was in charge of the kitchens and dining area. Employees believe Verna is a warm and protective presence and most likely to appear when things are going wrong. She continues to take care of customers and sometimes follows employees to the basement storeroom, even in the afterlife.

Egg Harbor's ghosts don't limit themselves to businesses in town. They've been known to frequent at least one farmhouse on County Road T outside of town. Elizabeth and Matthias Ostrand had toiled on this small farm for many years and had raised their children there. In 1997, Matthias passed away. Elizabeth had never noticed anything odd until her husband died.

It started with a light in the chicken coop coming on after Elizabeth had turned it off. Even after having the coop rewired and a new switch installed, the light in the chicken coop seemed to have a mind of its own.

Then one night in bed, Elizabeth heard a familiar sound. The sound of nail clippers. Her husband had had a habit of using them just before bedtime. Turning on the light, she watched the nail clippers bounce around on the night table before falling to the floor.

Elizabeth couldn't believe her eyes. The next morning, she went to see her daughter and granddaughter who lived nearby. They didn't think she was imagining things. Instead, they shared their own unusual stories of similar experiences in the farmhouse. Not knowing what to do, Elizabeth

just ignored the chicken coop light and put the nail clippers in a drawer.

A few weeks later, Elizabeth was awakened again. This time it was by a female voice. Sitting at the foot of her bed was a woman in old-fashioned rag curlers. Women used to wind their hair around pieces of rags before bedtime. They woke up the next day with curly hair. The rag-curl woman was sitting with her legs crossed, smoking a cigarette. She was laughing and talking, although Elizabeth couldn't make out what she was saying. After a few more visits, the woman stopped coming around.

More than a year later, Elizabeth came downstairs to find a half-eaten can of beans on the kitchen counter. The lid was jagged and still attached. She called her children to see if anyone had come by. No one had. There were no other signs of an intruder. It happened two more times. The third time, she heard a man's laugh. She turned to see a man's face in a cubbyhole next to the cabinet. He had dark hair and a beard.

Elizabeth said, "You're welcome to food, but please don't waste it. And clean up when you're done!" With that the spirit disappeared.

Elizabeth died in in 2002, and the property is now deserted. So we can't be sure whether or not the ghosts still haunt the chicken coop and the farmhouse. But if they do, perhaps Elizabeth has joined them . . .

Restless Resort

In the early 1920s, Jacob "Jac" Schmitz lived in Milwaukee with his wife, Sophie, and daughter, Irene. They owned a restaurant. But whenever they could get away, they would go to Baileys Harbor in Door County. They loved the natural beauty of the area so much that they bought land and built a cabin north of the old Baileys Harbor Life-Saving Station.

When Sophie died unexpectedly in 1925, Jac and Irene moved to their cabin in Baileys Harbor.

Jac and his younger brother, George, began talking about opening a summer resort there. George joined them in Baileys Harbor, and construction began on cabins, a dining room, and an office.

In 1935, Schmitz Gazebos opened. While Jac and George played hosts, Irene worked behind the scenes to keep things running smoothly.

The resort was a success. Guests returned year after year. Unfortunately, Jac died five years after its opening. George and Irene continued running the resort. It was a lot of work, but they enjoyed it. The cabins stayed full every summer.

When George died in 1965, he left everything to his niece. Irene was now sixty-one. She knew the resort was too much work for just her. With a sad heart, she sold the resort to Chicago lawyer Bert Wild. She moved to a red-and-white house at the south end of the property.

As successful as Schmitz Gazebos had been, Wild had plans to make it better. He wanted to attract millionaires. He started by renaming it Baileys

Harbor Yacht Club Resort. Then he built a massive building next to the lake. The building housed the new lobby, office, and a fancy dining room. This elegant building featured a huge fireplace and a circular staircase that led to an observation tower.

Yachts could pull up to the building from the harbor. Or guests could fly in on their private helicopters, landing at the new helicopter pad. Baileys Harbor Yacht Club became popular with the rich and famous. Ray Kroc, the man who started McDonald's, was a frequent guest.

But when Irene looked out her window, she could no longer see the harbor. All she could see was the enormous lodge and the giant yachts. If that wasn't bad enough, the annoying sounds of helicopters disturbed her peace and quiet.

Irene complained. Wild offered to pick up and move her house, but she didn't want to move. She wanted the peaceful, scenic harbor she had once known. She frequently said that she wished the main building would just burn to the ground.

Irene didn't get her wish while she was alive. But on a cold February morning in 1992, ten months after she had died at the age of eighty-eight, the Baileys Harbor Yacht Club Resort caught fire. There was serious damage, but fortunately no one was injured.

That evening, townspeople were talking about the fire at a local hangout. Suddenly, television programming was interrupted with news that the Baileys Harbor Yacht Club Resort was in flames. Again?

The townspeople were confused. Had the television station mistakenly aired the morning news? Somebody looked out the window. The night sky was orange, and it looked like flames were licking the moon. The fire department rushed past, sirens blaring. There was a firestorm at the resort. Angry flames shot out windows, refusing to be extinguished until the building was nothing but ashes.

Irene had gotten her wish. So did she have something to do with the mysterious fire that refused to go out? The red-and-white house still stands, and since the owners decided not to rebuild the main building, it has a better view than it once had.

But the story doesn't end here. The owners did build condos at the north end of the property. Most of the condos are rented to tourists in the summer and fall months. Owners come during the off season when things are slow, usually in the winter.

Year-round, a staffed front desk takes care of things. Everyone is required to check in so that staff knows who is in residence in case of an emergency.

One winter night, an assistant manager named Matt was on duty. He was startled by the ringing of the front desk phone. He answered it but heard only a low moaning, almost a growl. Matt looked at the display on the phone. The call was coming from an empty condo.

"Hello? Hello? Is anybody there?" Matt asked.

Worried that someone forgot to check in and was in trouble, he rushed to the unit with his master keys. But it was dark, quiet, and empty.

Matt returned to the front desk, confused. Minutes later, the phone rang again. This time, he heard breathing. The display showed the call coming from another unit that was also supposed to be empty. Once again he rushed out to check the condo. No one was there. He searched the property, and even checked the phone box. He could find no explanation for the mysterious phone calls.

The next morning, he told the manager what happened. The manager called the phone company and asked them to check the equipment. They did and reported that everything was working as it should be.

However, that night, it happened to Matt again. He wondered if someone was playing a prank but couldn't figure out how they were doing it. He reported the calls again. Then there were a couple of quiet nights before the calls happened a third time. This time, someone else was on duty.

The phone company again checked the equipment, finding nothing. The calls continued. Sounds ranged from a low growl to breathing and sometimes even muffled laughter. And they always happened late at night. Then the few condo owners who were in residence began to receive the same type of calls.

An angry manager called the phone company a third time. He insisted they change the equipment. He could think of no other reason for the disturbing late night phone calls. The phone company did as he asked.

The phone calls stopped . . . for a while. And you guessed it, they started up again. Now, the resort just accepts that the ghostly phone calls will happen from time to time. They stop, and just when you think they've stopped for good, they start again.

Now who do you think might be responsible for these ghostly phone calls?

Ghostly Animals

We've talked about ghostly people, ships, bicycles, and cars. What about animals? Yes, there are animal ghosts too. Many seem to have a purpose in remaining behind. And then there's Calf 1781.

Wisconsin, including Door County, is known for its dairy farms. One day, a young farm worker named Leslie was feeding the calves at one of those dairy farms. After she poured the grain into the pens, all the calves rushed up to eat. All except one. Number 1781. This calf just hung back.

Part of a dairy worker's job was to report possible illness or problems. Leslie was pretty sure this calf had suffered from pneumonia before. She watched the calf. The calf stared at Leslie with its big sad eyes. Other than not eating, the calf didn't seem in distress, so Leslie left.

The next day, Leslie fed the calves again. This time, there was no sign of Calf 1781. Leslie asked the boss if something had happened to her. The boss looked it up on his computer. Calf 1781 had died two weeks earlier.

To our knowledge, Calf 1781 hasn't been seen again. Did it miss home? Perhaps it didn't know where to go.

Other incidents show animals repaying the kindness humans have shown them, like . . . the man on Washington Island who made sure the songbirds around his home always had food and a place to perch in spring and summer. The songbirds migrated to warmer places during winter.

One particularly cold day, this man and a friend were returning from the mainland, driving their car across the ice. Halfway into their journey, the car got stuck. The men had no choice but to walk. As they made their way back, a blinding blizzard struck. They could only see a few feet in front of them. The marked path was getting buried by snow. The men were in danger of getting lost or taking a misstep off the ice into the freezing lake.

Suddenly, a songbird appeared. It chirped, flew a few feet, and landed. As the men reached the bird, it did the same thing. They continued following the bird across the ice. When they reached the island, the summer songbird vanished.

Another Door County family reports being saved from a fire by Buster, their Labrador retriever. You can probably find hundreds of stories of dogs saving people from fires. The difference in this story is that Buster had been dead for nine months.

One night, the parents were asleep in their upstairs bedroom. The children were in a downstairs bedroom. An electrical problem led to a fire in the family room. The father was awakened by whining and barking from Buster. Because of this, the family was able to get to safety.

Buster remained a loyal companion, even after his death.

We hope you enjoyed this trip through Door County and the ghosts you've met. Maybe you'll get to visit in person soon. If you do, keep your eyes and ears open. You never know what you might come across on a mist-covered lake, a spooky old lighthouse, or a deserted road.

Karen Bush Gibson has written dozens of children's books on many different subjects. She writes about people, places, and history because she loves research. Gibson is a member of the Society of Children's Book Writers and Illustrators.

Check out some of the other Spooky America titles available now!

Spooky America was adapted from the creeptastic Haunted America series, for adults. Haunted America explores historical haunts in cities and regions across America. Each book chronicles both the widely known and less-familiar history behind local ghosts and other unexplained mysteries. Here's more from the original *Haunted Door County* author Gayle Soucek:

www.gaylesoucek.com